C000138551

THE LITTLE BOOK OF

VODKA

TIPS

Andrew Langley

THE LITTLE BOOK OF

VODKA

TIPS

BLOOMSBURY ABSOLUTE
LONDON · OXFORD · NEW YORK · NEW DELHI · SYDNEY

'After a glass of vodka you are no longer Peter Sorin, but Peter Sorin and somebody else. Your ego splits in two.'

Anton Chekhov,
The Seagull

1.

Vodka breaks a lot of rules. It has no colour, and often little flavour (its Slavic name means 'little water'). It can be made anywhere, using a wide array of ingredients and it is rarely aged. Yet **vodka is one of the world's great spirits, capable of surprising us with its subtlety and character**.

"Vodka is one of the world's great spirits, capable of surprising us with its subtlety and character."

2. Exploring vodka #1: neutral.

Vodka is produced in many different ways, each of which can create a distinct identity. The most familiar is 'neutral' vodka, which has – deliberately – no flavour or aroma at all. This is the most popular vodka for cocktails and other mixed drinks.

"Exploring vodka #1: neutral."

3. Thanks to James Bond, the vodka Martini has mythic status. **For the 007 experience, put crushed ice, a shot of vodka and** 1 teaspoon of **French vermouth in a shaker and shake well**. Otherwise, simply stir the same ingredients. Serve with a twist of lemon rind or 3 olives.

" For the 007 experience, put crushed ice, a shot of vodka and French vermouth in a shaker and shake well. "

4. **Quince vodka preserves the fruit's exotic charm.** Wash and grate 2 quinces (peel and all) into a 1 litre Kilner jar. Add 60g of sugar, then top up with vodka. Close, seal and leave for about 3 months in a dark place, shaking regularly. Strain off into a bottle ready for use.

"Quince vodka preserves the fruit's exotic charm."

5. Neutral vodka is just ripe for flavouring – and it's dead easy to do it yourself. **One of the simplest flavoured vodkas uses vanilla pods. Slice the pods lengthways and pop them into a bottle of vodka to infuse.** Leave for a month, turning occasionally, then test the result.

"One of the simplest flavoured vodkas uses vanilla pods. Slice the pods lengthways and pop them into a bottle of vodka to infuse."

6. Here's an astounding taste combination. Marinate salmon or halibut steaks in lemon juice, oil and 15ml of grated horseradish root for 30 minutes. Steam the fish over a pan containing 180ml of simmering vodka for 10 minutes. **Boil down the vodka, whisking in more horseradish and 180ml of sour cream to make a delicious sauce**.

"Boil down the vodka, whisking in horseradish and sour cream to make a delicious sauce."

7. Allegedly named after a Los Angeles surfer, **the Harvey Wallbanger was a cult drink in the 1970s**. It is, in fact, a souped-up Screwdriver. To make it, **pour** 3 parts **vodka over ice, cover with** a float of 1 part **Galliano and top up with orange juice**.

"The Harvey Wallbanger was a cult drink in the 1970s. Pour vodka over ice, cover with Galliano and top up with orange juice."

8. **A premium vodka deserves to be sipped with care** rather than necked in one. To get the most from the experience, use a small, heavy-bottomed tumbler or, better still, a tulip-shaped glass with a round bowl and a narrow opening. These will concentrate the spirit's aromas.

"A premium vodka deserves to be sipped with care."

9. With vodka, **smell is just as important as taste**. Pour a shot of vodka, swirl the liquid and lower your nose gently towards the glass. Inhale rather than sniff, with your mouth open. You should get a range of delicate aromas. If your nostrils sting uncomfortably, it's a low-grade vodka.

"Smell is just as important as taste.

10.

Add zing to pork chops with a vodka apple sauce. For the sauce, heat a little oil in a pan and sauté 2 onions and 4 apples, peeled, chopped and cored. Add 2 tablespoons of cider vinegar, plus sage, thyme and salt. Cook the pork chops, then flambé in 60ml of vodka. Remove the meat and stir the sauce into the vodka.

"Add zing to pork chops with a vodka apple sauce...

11.

Exploring vodka #2: wheat.
Wheat vodkas are produced all
over the world, from England to
Russia, and from Sweden to New
Zealand. The wheat imparts
a subtle peppery flavour, with
hints of fennel and lemon. Drink
wheat and other grain vodkas
with savoury dishes from
Eastern Europe.

"Exploring vodka #2: wheat."

12.

The Screwdriver is a classic vodka cocktail with a hundred variations – plus added Vitamin C. Here's the (ridiculously simple) basic recipe. Just take a highball glass, put in ice and a shot of vodka, then top with orange juice to taste. Chuck in a slice of orange.

"The Screwdriver is a classic vodka cocktail with a hundred variations."

13.

Always begin by sipping a fine vodka neat. Mixers, fruit juices and ice are going to get in the way of the real taste – obviously. But after a few sips and rollings, add a little plain water. **Adding water can bring out yet more flavours by releasing compounds in the spirit.**

"Adding water can bring out yet more flavours by releasing compounds in the spirit."

14.

What food goes best with vodka?
Basically, anything strong and acid will click perfectly. Smoked fish, sausage and ham match up a treat, plus salty things like caviar (of course). Accompany with pickled beetroot, cucumber, radishes and sauerkraut, plus pumpernickel and cream cheese.

"What food goes best with vodka?

15.

A Bloody Mary gives you (almost all) your five a day in one cocktail. In a tall glass with ice, mix 45ml of vodka, 100ml of tomato juice, 1 teaspoon each of Worcester Sauce, horseradish sauce and lemon juice, and pinches of pepper and salt. Serve with a stick of celery and a slice of lemon.

"A Bloody Mary gives you (almost all) your five a day in one cocktail."

16. **Vodka sauce transforms shrimp pasta.** Simply brown a chopped onion and a garlic clove in butter with a sprinkle of chilli flakes. Add a can of tomato passata, with 60ml of vodka, 90ml of double cream and the zest of a lemon. Put in 450g of raw shrimps and cook for 5 minutes. Serve with fettucine.

"Vodka sauce transforms shrimp pasta."

17. For a real taste of 1980s New York, **make your own Cosmopolitan: shake up** 2 parts neutral **vodka with** 2 parts **Cointreau,** 3 parts **cranberry juice,** 1 part **fresh lime juice, ice and a dash of Angostura Bitters**. Strain into a chilled glass and top with a twist of (lightly) flamed orange peel.

"Make your own Cosmopolitan: shake up vodka with Cointreau, cranberry juice, fresh lime juice, ice and a dash of Angostura Bitters."

18. **Exploring vodka #3: potato.** The humble spud brings a creamy and slightly vegetabley taste to the spirit, and gives a heavier texture than grain. It can be a bit earthy and harsh on its own but is perfect for cocktails which need a hint of added sweetness.

"**Exploring vodka #3: potato.**"

19.

Where should you keep your vodka?
Unopened bottles can be stored in a cool, dry place. They should be well away from direct sunlight, which can speed up the evaporation of alcohol and cause chemical changes in the spirit, spoiling the taste. Store upright, to prevent any leakage.

"Where should you keep your vodka?

20.

Krupnik is a honey and vodka liqueur much loved in Poland and Belarus. **Make your own *Krupnik* by gently warming** 700g of **honey in a pan with** 3 **cloves,** 1 **allspice berry,** 1 **cinnamon stick,** half a **vanilla pod and lemon zest**. **Stir in** 450ml of **vodka** and let it cool. Strain into bottles. Serve warm.

"Make your own *Krupnik* by gently warming honey in a pan with cloves, allspice berry, cinnamon stick, vanilla pod and lemon zest. Stir in vodka."

21. The legendary Espresso Martini contains no Martini, but it needs a conical Martini glass. **For this iconic cocktail, shake up 45ml of vodka with 20ml of Kahlúa or Tia Maria, 30ml of hot fresh espresso coffee, ice and a pinch of salt.** Strain into the glass and pop 4 coffee beans on top (which should be foamy).

"For this iconic cocktail, shake up 45ml of vodka with 20ml of Kahlúa or Tia Maria, 30ml of hot fresh espresso coffee, ice and a pinch of salt."

22. **Drink vodka like a Russian!** In fact, this means making it part of a meal. Between each shot of spirit, Russians eat small portions of food, rather like Spanish tapas. These snacks, called *zakuski*, include cold meats, cured fish, pickled vegetables and stuffed dumplings.

"**Drink vodka like a Russian!**"

23.

Zubrowka **is a classic flavoured vodka from Poland**. Rye vodka is flavoured with extract of bison grass, which adds a yellow tinge and a unique taste that includes cut grass, lavender and black pepper. *Zubrowka* is **often served with apple juice, or even poured over vanilla ice cream**.

"*Zubrowka* **is a classic flavoured vodka from Poland, often served with apple juice, or even poured over vanilla ice cream."**

24.

Here's yet another great match for vodka – chocolate! The Chocolate Martini is just sweet enough. Wipe cocoa round the rim of a glass. Shake up a shot of vodka with the same of chocolate liqueur such as Crème de Cacao and ice. Strain into a glass and add fragments of good milk chocolate.

"Here's yet another great match for vodka – chocolate!"

25. Despite its name, **the Moscow Mule is an unmistakeably American cocktail**. It even has its own special copper mug, though a glass is just as good. **Pour in a slug of vodka, squeeze half a lime on top, add ice, then top up with good ginger beer.** Serve with a lime slice.

"The Moscow Mule is an unmistakeably American cocktail. Pour in a slug of vodka, squeeze half a lime on top, add ice, then top up with good ginger beer."

26. **Vodka makes an excellent cleaning liquid** about the house. Soak a cloth in the stuff and use it to wipe down china ornaments and glass or plastic light fittings. Or dilute it with 3 parts water to make a chemical-free spray for polishing up your windows.

"Vodka makes an excellent cleaning liquid."

27.

How long will an opened bottle of vodka last? Once the seal is broken, it should be good for up to six months, so long as you screw the top back on firmly. But oxygen will still get in, causing the alcohol to evaporate. A tight cork or a hinged plastic stopper may give a better seal.

"How long will an opened bottle of vodka last?"

28. **The vodka cure – for fish.** Whizz up 75g each of salt and sugar, 40g of fresh dill, 10g of fresh tarragon, 3g of fennel seed, 250g of peeled raw beetroot and 2 shots of vodka. Pour this over 4 salmon or herring fillets. Cover and refrigerate for 30 hours, turning the fish over halfway through.

"The vodka cure – for fish."

29. Here's another brilliant vodka and fish match. Oil a heavy pan and sear 4 steaks of firm white fish such as hake or halibut (3 minutes a side). Remove the steaks and put in a hot oven. **Deglaze the pan with the juice of a lime plus** 60ml of **vodka, adding butter and capers. Pour over the fish to serve.**

"Deglaze the pan with the juice of a lime plus vodka, adding butter and capers. Pour over the fish to serve."

30. **A Vodka Tonic** is just what it says – vodka with tonic and ice. And very nice too. But it **can be jazzed up with simple touches**. Serve with a slice of lime and a few mint leaves. Pop in a few fresh cranberries, plus maybe a drop of cranberry juice or mango liqueur.

"A Vodka Tonic can be jazzed up with simple touches."

31. **Exploring vodka #4: rye.** Rye vodka is the revered national drink of Poland. This grain adds a dry, nutty element to vodka – with the bonus of spicy, menthol traces. It's good for sipping neat, or for cocktails based on vegetable (rather than fruit) flavours, such as a Bloody Mary.

"Exploring vodka #4: rye."

32. **Beef with vodka? Yes, it really works.** Take a fine rib of beef and stud it with bay leaves stuffed into slits. Rub all over with a mix of vodka, salt and pepper and leave for 3 hours. Roast in a good hot oven in your preferred manner. The gravy will be sensational.

Beef with vodka? Yes, it really works.

33.

Soothe those aches and stings with vodka. **Got an aching tooth? Sluice the affected area with a sip of neat vodka.** The alcohol will disinfect and soothe at the same time. The same goes for nettle, poison ivy and even jellyfish stings – so carry vodka wherever you go!

"Got an aching tooth? Sluice the affected area with a sip of neat vodka.

34. **What could be more warming than vodka soup?** Gently roast 1kg of ripe tomatoes with 2 chopped red peppers, 3 chopped onions and a garlic clove, plus oil, for 1 hour. Blitz them all in a processor (in batches), with 60ml of vodka and a slug of Worcester Sauce. Strain and stir in cream to suit.

"What could be more warming than vodka soup?"

35. **The first sip of a fine vodka is a magic moment, so take it easy.** Take in enough to cover your tongue and roll it round your mouth. As the alcohol evaporates, you will feel the texture and taste the first hints of what could be a host of flavours. Try to identify as many as you can.

"The first sip of a fine vodka is a magic moment, so take it easy."

36. Real vodka stays liquid in a freezer. That's why **it's fine** – though not compulsory – **to chill a bottle in the freezer for at most 2 hours before drinking it**. The intense cold thickens the vodka's texture and makes it more viscous, adding a whole new dimension to the mouth feel.

"It's fine to chill a bottle in the freezer for at most 2 hours before drinking it."

37. **Vodka plus pasta plus seafood never disappoints.** Fry up a large chopped onion plus some garlic in oil, adding 2 handfuls of chopped chorizo. After 10 minutes, add 170ml of vodka and about 36 well-cleaned clams. Cover and steam for 5 minutes. Stir in with cooked linguine and chopped parsley.

"Vodka plus pasta plus seafood never disappoints."

38.

A dash of vodka produces the flakiest pastry ever. The spirit stops the gluten in the flour from breaking down, and makes the end result more tender and crumbly. **Replace 2 tablespoons of water with the same of ice-cold vodka when mixing the dough for a pie crust.**

"Replace 2 tablespoons of water with the same of ice-cold vodka when mixing the dough for a pie crust."

39.

A Black Russian dramatically combines a colourless spirit with something black and opaque. Sling some ice cubes in a tumbler. Then pour over 5 parts vodka and 2 parts coffee liqueur, such as Kahlúa or Tia Maria. For a White Russian, add cream.

"A Black Russian dramatically combines a colourless spirit with something black and opaque."

40. Oat and honey vodka is as good as it sounds and simple to make. **Combine 260g of raw honey,** 200g of **rolled oats and** 1 litre of **good wheat vodka in a large preserving jar**. Seal and keep in the refrigerator for 5 days, shaking it every day. Then strain through muslin into a bottle.

"Combine raw honey, rolled oats and good wheat vodka in a large preserving jar."

41. Learn a few authentic Russian toasts to go with your vodka. *Vashi zdarovye!* means 'Good health!' (to a group of people). *Za nashoo drooshboo!* means 'To our friendship!'. And *Na pasashok!* means 'One for the road!' (Be aware that *Nastravia!* is not a toast at all.)

"Learn a few authentic Russian toasts: *Vashi zdarovye! Za nashoo drooshboo! Na pasashok!*"

42. **Spicy Vodka Bitters make terrific cocktails** (as a starting point, try with sherry and elderflower). To make your own, infuse 225ml of vodka with 2 dessertspoons of cardamom seeds, lightly crushed. After 5 days, strain out the cardamom and replace with 1 dessertspoon of saffron threads. A day after that, strain the vodka again.

"Spicy Vodka Bitters make terrific cocktails."

43.

For a comforting dessert, whip up a vodka butterscotch pudding. Melt 60g of butter, then stir in 150g of brown sugar and 225ml of cream. Simmer and stir until it thickens. In a bowl, whisk 2 tablespoons of cornflour with 375ml of milk and 3 egg yolks, then slowly stir in the butterscotch sauce. Heat it all up again and mix in a shot of vodka. Chill.

"For a comforting dessert, whip up a vodka butterscotch pudding...

44. Like its name, **a Seabreeze cocktail is perfect for a hot summer's day**. In a highball glass, stir together ice, 1 part vodka, 1 part grapefruit juice and 2 parts cranberry juice. Garnish with a slice of lime. For variety, try using a flavoured vodka.

"**A Seabreeze cocktail is perfect for a hot summer's day.**"

45. **Exploring vodka #5: corn.** Gluten intolerant? Most grain and potato vodkas won't be suitable for you, but maize vodka could be the answer. There is now a growing range available, many distilled in the southern USA. The corn produces a smooth and buttery texture.

"Exploring vodka #5: corn."

46. **You can happily infuse vodka with almost anything.** Here are some of the whackier ideas which work successfully. Smoked salmon shreds and lemon zest; cooked bacon (yes, really – some people use only the fat); raw peeled garlic and habanero chilli; tomato; toffee; a Mars Bar.

"You can happily infuse vodka with almost anything."

47. Here's a recipe **for a super quick, super simple vodka ice cream**. **Put** 75ml of **good vodka in a food processor with** 600ml of **very good vanilla ice cream and** 1 dessertspoon of **grated coconut.** Whizz up, transfer to a plastic tub and leave in the freezer overnight.

"For a super quick, super simple vodka ice cream, put good vodka in a food processor with very good vanilla ice cream and grated coconut."

48.

Q: Who hates vodka? A: Insects do. In fact, it's the alcohol they don't like, which means **vodka is a highly effective insect-repellent (with no propellants or nasty chemicals involved)**. A few dabs of vodka will keep midges, mosquitoes and other flying pests at bay.

"Vodka is a highly effective insect-repellent (with no propellants or nasty chemicals involved).

49.

Vodka and chocolate make a sublime mousse. Melt 350g of dark chocolate, 60g of butter and shots of vodka and Baileys. When cool, add 60ml of whipping cream with 1 teaspoon of gelatine. Beat another 340ml of cream with 45ml of sugar and a dash of vanilla essence. Fold into the chocolate mix and chill.

"Vodka and chocolate make a sublime mousse. "

50. **Wash your hair with vodka!** Diluted, of course. Pour a shot into your bottle of shampoo and shake gently to mix. The purity and low alkalinity of the spirit helps to get rid of frizz and add a shine to your tresses.

"Wash your hair with vodka!"

Andrew Langley

Andrew Langley is **a knowledgeable food and drink writer.** Among his formative influences he lists a season picking grapes in Bordeaux, several years of raising sheep and chickens in Wiltshire and two decades drinking his grandmother's tea. He has written books on a number of Scottish and Irish whisky distilleries and is the editor of the highly regarded anthology of the writings of the legendary Victorian chef Alexis Soyer.

"A knowledgeable food and drink writer."

**Little Books of Tips from
Bloomsbury Absolute**

Aga	Gin
Allotment	Golf
Avocado	Herbs
Beer	Prosecco
Cake Decorating	Rum
Cheese	Spice
Cider	Tea
Coffee	Vodka
Fishing	Whisky
Gardening	Wine

If you enjoyed this book, try...

THE LITTLE BOOK OF

RUM

TIPS

"For legendary Bananas Foster, melt together butter, dark sugar and cinnamon. Stir in banana liqueur, add bananas and fry. Flambé in a shot of gold rum."

"Essential rum cocktail #1: the Mojito."

BLOOMSBURY ABSOLUTE
Bloomsbury Publishing Plc
50 Bedford Square, London, WC1B 3DP, UK

BLOOMSBURY, BLOOMSBURY ABSOLUTE, the Diana logo and the Absolute Press
logo are trademarks of Bloomsbury Publishing Plc

First published in Great Britain 2019
Copyright © Andrew Langley, 2019
Cover image © Matt Inwood, 2019

A catalogue record for this book is available from the British Library.
Library of Congress Cataloguing-in-Publication data has been applied for.

ISBN: 9781472973337
2 4 6 8 10 9 7 5 3 1

Printed and bound in China by Toppan Leefung Printing

Bloomsbury Publishing Plc makes every effort to ensure that the papers used in the
manufacture of our books are natural, recyclable products made from wood grown in
well-managed forests. Our manufacturing processes conform to the environmental
regulations of the country of origin.

To find out more about our authors and books visit www.bloomsbury.com and sign
up for our newsletters.